917.91   Elmer

Arizona in color.   138468

Date Due

MAR 1 1 1989			
3-25			
4-8			
JAN 2 8 1992			
APR 2 9 2000			
NOV 1 6 2002			
MAY 2 7 2009			

BRODART, INC.   Cat. No. 23 233   Printed in U.S.A.

Sat. 9:00 A.M.—5:30 P.M.

ARIZONA
IN COLOR

ARIZONA
in Color

by

CARLOS H. ELMER

HASTINGS HOUSE · PUBLISHERS

New York, 10016

PUBLISHED 1973 BY HASTINGS HOUSE, PUBLISHERS, INC.

Published simultaneously in Canada by
Saunders, of Toronto, Ltd., Don Mills, Ontario

Library of Congress Cataloging in Publication Data

Elmer, Carlos H., *Arizona in Color*

(Profiles of America)
1. Arizona—Description and travel—Views.
I. Title.

F815.E42   917.91'04'50222   73–13945
ISBN 0–8038–0358–3

Printed and bound in England by Bookprint International

CONTENTS

Arizona, a Young State on Ancient Terrain

Arizona is one of the latest, and perhaps last great demonstrations of nature yielding to the energies of man. It lay there for billions of years, a vast sunbaked land of sandy deserts, barren hills, rivers that raged in flood in the spring and dried into rocky channels in the fall. It was a land where early visitors carried pickaxes and harvested minerals from the unfriendly soil, but where those who followed sought repose in the quiet valleys and wellbeing in the unsullied air. Arizona began to bloom when its people learned how to dam its waters and turn its desert into gardens and pastures.

What follows is the story of its growing expansion, its good roads, its cities rising with the influx of fresh capital, its people, coming by car and plane to stay. Sometimes the men of the older communities shake their heads at the procession of newcomers, wondering whether quantity will overwhelm nature's bounty. But there are still unharmed, the greatest wonders—the Grand Canyon of the Colorado, the fantastic peaks of sunlit stone, the deep changing colors of the twilights.

I

ARIZONA'S 113,810 square miles have seen a bewildering assortment of residents and visitors since man first arrived. Most mysterious of all were the Hohokam People, the "Ancient Ones," who enjoyed a flourishing civilization in central Arizona for centuries and then suddenly vanished. They left evidences of a sophisticated system of irrigation canals and ditches, plus a unique four-story "skyscraper" on the flat desert floor, Casa Grande, "the Big House."

Gone were the Hohokam when Spaniards first came from Mexico in search of non-existent golden cities of Cibola. The Spaniards were met by the Papago Indians who first experienced contact with the arms and religion of Spain in this region. A remarkable legacy remains near Tucson—Mission San Xavier del Bac, serving the Papago as a spiritual home now as it has since 1797.

Spanish soldiers and priests combined to explore this vast and uncharted territory that was shown on their maps as a blank area named *Pimeria Alta*. In 1776, as the founding fathers met in far-off Philadelphia, a notable man of the cloth, Fr. Francisco Garces, first visited the Havasupai Indians in their Grand Canyon home. American wanderers were not far behind, both individual adventurers and members of organized military expeditions. The fearsome depths of the Grand Canyon first yielded their secrets to a brave one-armed veteran of the Civil War and his followers, while a young officer of the U.S. Navy led a strange caravan of camels across the desert in search of new routes to the Pacific. Beset by the elements and Apaches, prospectors and ranchers fought for a foothold in this alien land.

They came in small bands and they came alone. Their presence went almost unnoticed in this huge and lonely land. Rails forged links across the continent, but to Arizona they brought only tiny watering stops that hardly made up for loss of the Butterfield Stage depots. By 1900 there were but 123,000 souls in the entire Territory, hardly the population of an obscure suburb of Los Angeles today. There was, in fact, just about a full square mile for every man, woman, and babe in arms.

Most of the Arizonans at the dawn of a bright, new century were here to wrest mineral wealth from the rugged hills. A rich torrent of gold and silver came from Tombstone, the Vulture at Wickenburg, Oatman's Tom Reed, and other famous producers. The huge mountains of copper ore that now account for the bulk of Arizona's mineral production were overlooked in those frantic days, and almost as a minor sideshow attraction, a few farmers tilled flat lands of the Salt River Valley around a town named for the legendary Phoenix bird. The land was rich, but lack of a dependable water supply made farming a gamble on a par with faro and poker.

II

IN 1911, just one year prior to statehood, came the big break—the completion of Roosevelt Dam, the first major project of the new Federal Bureau of Reclamation. Snow waters and storm floods on the watershed of the Salt River were captured and controlled for the first time. Canals and ditches in the Salt River Valley could be expanded with assurance water would be there when needed and that violent floods would never again wash them away. As additional dams were constructed on the Salt and Verde rivers, Phoenix and its valley blossomed as a major agricultural area blessed with bumper crops and a year round growing season.

Arizona began to grow up, with Phoenix as its main center of commerce and industry. The automobile arrived on the scene, but primitive roads tended to keep the huge state in widely separated portions. Cities like Yuma and Kingman on the west had much closer ties to Los Angeles than to Phoenix. Towns in the desolate northern part were cut off from regular contact with major centers of population, and could be reached from Phoenix only by long and rough roads.

With World War II's demand for the training of thousands of pilots in an area of sunny skies came Arizona's big change. Many of these airmen came back to put down permanent roots in this desert land they had come to love, and industries of the new air age also chose Arizona. The rush was on. Population almost doubled from 1940 to 1950, then doubled again. Mining and farming continued to grow at a steady rate, but the explosive growth came in manufacturing, particularly electronics. And that other industry called tourism flourished.

Word of mouth advertising by the same young men who had trained in the state during the war helped promote vacation travel to Arizona. A lesser role was played by Arizona's state travel development organization, whose total annual budget would carry the program of Florida for perhaps ten days. But Arizona's secret weapon was a modest little monthly magazine started by the Arizona Highway Department in 1925 to pass along information regarding the state's expanding network of roads. In fact, Arizona's rising tourist and population curves parallel those of *Arizona Highways* circulation. Out of thirty-two state-sponsored magazines, *Arizona Highways* is far ahead in circulation and editorial quality, and its influence on Arizona's mushrooming growth has been enormous.

As is usually the case when a product or idea succeeds spectacularly, there was one person chiefly responsible—Raymond Carlson, editor from 1938 to 1971. The Highway Department thought it needed a new editor, and found Raymond at work in its own offices, busily engaged in tracking down off-highway gasoline users to investigate their claims for gas tax refunds. A job such as this was not unusual in 1938 for an honors graduate of Stanford, who had majored in classical languages, and it is a remarkable stroke of luck that a man with this background and ability with the written word could be given a crack at the magazine job.

Before the bugle called Carlson as a rifleman in World War II, he had

9

produced sixty sparkling issues combining smart black and white photo lay-outs with polished words of his own and the best of the Arizona W.P.A. Writers' Project. Gone by 1939 were advertisements for culverts, road graders, and other products purchased by the sponsoring Arizona Highway Department. From then on the only item advertised was Arizona.

By March 1946, the familiar byline of Raymond Carlson appeared once more on the masthead. For over thirty years the same team of Carlson as Editor and George Avey as Art Editor was on the job, producing a new look at this perplexing subject each month—a source of constant amazement to the Editor, who had been on the job for five months when he came to the horrifying realization that he had run out of things to say about Arizona!

Known now primarily for the quality of its vivid color photographs, *Arizona Highways* climaxes each year with a million-copy Christmas issue done completely in color. This "Arizona Christmas Card" is read in every nation in the world and people in foreign lands have become more familiar with Arizona than any other of our states. Any list of persons influencing Arizona's growth in post-war years must be headed by Raymond Carlson, and there is a long blank space before whoever may be Number Two.

III

WORLD WAR II's flight trainees, emergence of an electronics industry, taming of wild rivers, and an unusually persuasive state magazine contributed to 1970's census enumerators finding about 1,750,000 people in the state, or nearly sixteen for each square mile.

Arizona is divided into two main geographical areas—the hot cactus-covered desert lowlands, which is most of the world's image of Arizona, and an equally large hunk of extremely scenic real estate composed of high plateaus and pine forests. Since the major population centers are in the desert, the high country remains virtually wide open space.

Nearly eighty percent of the population is clustered in only two metro-politan areas, Phoenix and Tucson, and it is there that the cries of "enough!" are heard most strongly. Therein lie the problems of traffic jams, smog, and staggering cost of government. The small cities in the country, like Prescott, Douglas, Kingman, and Safford are still untouched by most big city problems. But new residents continue to stream into Phoenix and Tucson.

Tourists, too, tend to base their operations in the two major cities, especially during the winter "snowbird" season. Up to now they have been welcomed with eagerness, with new resorts and mobile home parks springing up to accommodate them. Many of these winter visitors are content to sit in the warm sun, get in a few rounds of golf each week, and scan the Phoenix newspapers hopefully for word of major blizzards back home—while the traveler and explorer types among them find scenic Arizona occupies them full time.

Some of the latter are grimly determined to visit all available National Parks and National Monuments, a big job in a state containing the most National Monuments in the nation. Naturally heading the list are the Grand Canyon and the Petrified Forest, the latter only recently elevated from "Monument" to "Park." Winter visitors find they have chosen the most favorable and uncrowded time to see these impressive examples of nature's handiwork in northern Arizona.

The Grand Canyon is a favorite of visitors from abroad, who appear to appreciate its grandeur a great deal more than most of the American tourists. One young American screeched his VW to a halt at Mohave Point, left his very pregnant wife in the car and dashed to the railing, spraying the Canyon left to right and up and down, with an 8mm movie camera. He leaped back behind the wheel with this stirring report: "Myrtle, I got the whole thing!" The Canyon does not yield its mystery that quickly nor that easily to photographers, most of whom later find they have battled the Canyon and lost.

Capsule descriptions of the Grand Canyon of the Colorado are seldom satisfactory. Even entire books written by skilled word craftsmen like Joseph Wood Krutch, are poor substitutes for the actual experience. After standing in line for a Fred Harvey meal at El Tovar Hotel or Bright Angel Lodge, you may be jostled around a bit by the crowd on the Rim, but your view of the Canyon confirms Mr. Krutch's comment: not only is there no human being in sight but there is no evidence that any human has ever been there.

While the gorge is the main attraction at Grand Canyon's South Rim, another feature would be worthy of a trip in its own right: In 1911 a pair of carefree and daredevil brothers, Emery and Ellsworth Kolb led wooden boat trips through the rapids of the Colorado River and made a motion picture of the journeys. Shown daily at Kolb Studio, a little cottage that hangs on the side of the canyon wall, the most fascinating aspect of this jerky and thoroughly scratched film is the narration, supplied not by a recording or callow attendant reading from notes, but by Emery Kolb in person. He modestly terms this "the longest run one man show in the world." I'm sure there are few other contenders.

Today hundreds or thousands, including grandmothers and small children, place themselves in the hands of commercial "river runners" each season to retrace the route of the Kolb brothers. Sixty years ago, though, it was different, as we learn from this genuine pioneer's Grand Canyon lore.

Arizona feels sufficiently strongly about the subject to include on license plates the notification that the car hails from the Grand Canyon State, just as Wisconsin proclaims itself America's Dairyland. So it is no small wonder that Arizonans sob and shake their fists at national magazines that print travel stories placing the Grand Canyon in the state of Colorado.

While the Grand Canyon of the Colorado (River) is pretty much a "look, don't touch" proposition for ninety-nine percent of the tourists who do not leave the Rim to go down trails on foot or by mule train, Oak Creek Canyon eighty miles to the south is another matter. Here the highway winds down a series of switchbacks and enters a wonderland of red and white cliffs, backdrops of some of Hollywood's most famous western movies, showing cowboys chasing Indians among the red rocks.

Oak Creek Canyon and its only town, Sedona, have been favorite vacation destinations for residents of Arizona since automobile roads first entered the canyon. Retired persons, artists, and others who wished to get away from it all have settled here, and now find they are being joined by far too many neighbors to fit comfortably in the confines of the canyon. Like the South Rim of the Grand Canyon with its narrow strip of civilization, Oak Creek Canyon is trying to cope with the problems that accompany an ever-increasing number of people attempting to crowd into a finite space. Despite its mini traffic jams Sedona continues to exude charm and allows one to admire a large canyon from the bottom looking up without leaving the comfort of an automobile.

After the Grand Canyon and Oak Creek Canyon, Arizona's third major red rock area is Monument Valley, a bizarre assortment of sandstone buttes and towers situated on the Arizona–Utah border. Some of its splendor can be seen from a passenger car, but most of it is hidden away down sandy trails that require use of a four-wheel-drive vehicle. Quite an extensive tour guide business has sprung up, for Monument Valley not only features extravagant scenery, but is also the home of many Navajo Indians. A tour from Goulding's Lodge, for example, invariably surprises visitors, introducing them to a people living with dignity and apparent content in a harsh land devoid of productivity. Navajo hogans are spotlessly clean, children play happily with their meagre toys, and adults talk freely about their way of life. Hogans far removed from tourist routes may not duplicate the showcase appearance of those seen on Monument Valley guided tours, but these people give a favorable impression, as people worthy of respect and assistance in finding a rightful place in this complex world.

Harry and "Mike" Goulding are the pioneer white residents of this part of the world—they put it on the map. In 1938, John Ford wanted to make another western starring John Wayne and Harry persuaded him to film it in Monument Valley. The result was the Oscar-winning *Stagecoach*. John Ford

12

returned many times to make more movies, even when the unusual background scenery of Monument Valley was not required, or was even inappropriate for the story's development. In those days a few hardy tourists braved rough and dusty roads to see the monuments, but it was only a few years ago that the area opened up with completion of a paved highway through the valley and development by the Navajo of a Tribal Park area.

Arizona's sixteen National Monuments and Petrified Forest National Park provide a remarkable assortment of historic lore and specialized scenic attraction, and there are many other spots of great scenic charm found in scattered locations throughout the state. But these big three—Grand Canyon, Oak Creek Canyon and Monument Valley, are Arizona's spectaculars, unlike anything else to be found in our land.

The man-made lakes that stretch like a string of jewels from Utah's border to southwestern Arizona's midsection are also worthy of special note. Each bears a name important to the Southwest, and each has its own distinctive character. The first is the newest, formed by Glen Canyon Dam and named for Major John Wesley Powell, heroic conqueror of the Colorado River. Lake Powell backs into red rock canyons and grottoes well up into Utah, coming within an easy stroll of Rainbow Bridge National Monument. The contrast of deep red walls and blue waters seen from your boat tour is a striking one. Yet this peaceful and beautiful scene masks a bitter dispute that has raged for a decade between conservationists and dam builders.

An elegant color book, *The Place No One Knows*, shows Glen Canyon as it was before the lake formed, and mourns the passing of the beautiful, tranquil scenes a few hundred river runners saw each year before construction of Glen Canyon Dam. The protest became so great that the proposed Bridge Canyon Dam north of Peach Springs, Arizona was essentially blocked on the grounds that its lake would flood the Grand Canyon. An intense campaign included bumper stickers asking, "Would you flood the Sistine Chapel to get closer to the ceiling?" To take its place in supplying electrical energy to feed the boundless maw of Southern California, huge coal-fired power plants are rising in our desert land, plants that California won't permit within its borders because of air pollution standards! The conservation score is in doubt.

Next and downstream is the first and biggest, Lake Mead, formed by Hoover Dam. Named for Dr. Elwood Mead, Commissioner of Reclamation from 1924 to 1936, the huge lake stretches far into the lower end of the Grand Canyon by the Grand Wash Cliffs, a distance of more than 115 miles from the dam. As Hoover Dam was being constructed a great debate raged over the lake's effect on the area's climate. Learned estimates ranged from no difference at all to a veritable Garden of Eden in a desert land. Huge as Lake Mead is, the former was true.

As cold, clear waters of the Colorado River emerge from the Hoover Dam power plant, they almost immediately slow up in the upper reaches of Lake Mohave. Named for Mohave County, Arizona, and the Mohave Indians, this narrow lake stretches sixty-five miles through forbidding Black Canyon, past a major trout hatchery at Willow Beach, and ends at Davis Dam, west of Kingman. Water drawn into Hoover Dam from several hundred feet under the surface of Lake Mead emerges at fifty-two degrees Fahrenheit, ideal for rainbow trout. It is one of the strange aspects of this desert lake that trout survive and flourish at a spot where summer air temperatures regularly exceed 110 degrees.

The Colorado River's last big lake is formed by Parker Dam and is named Lake Havasu, an Indian name meaning "blue-green water." This warm water lake supplies the major part of Los Angeles' drinking water, and will soon furnish additional waters to central Arizona through a complex system of aqueducts and tunnels named the Central Arizona Project. It is Arizona's home for the London Bridge, which has been erected over a lake channel as part of a new planned community development.

In less than forty years the northern and western boundaries of Arizona formed by the Colorado River have been transformed from an ugly, sullen and often destructive area into one of great beauty and benefit. None of us who have watched this transformation take place is apologetic for the changes wrought and we would advocate additional projects of this type.

The three red rock areas and the chain of desert lakes may symbolize Arizona's scenic greatness but the remainder of the state is not lacking. Especially in spring, the cactus-filled deserts of southern Arizona have great charm: Organ Pipe Cactus National Monument, near the Mexican border; Pinal Pioneer Parkway, near Florence; and Joshua Tree Parkway, north of Wickenburg. Equally enjoyable are the pine forests and meadows of the high country: Kaibab National Forest at Grand Canyon's North Rim, the White Mountains of eastern Arizona, and the highlands along US 666, the Coronado Trail, which goes south of Alpine near the New Mexico border.

Yes, there is scenery aplenty. The reproductions in *Arizona Highways* are faithful, despite some objections from the Soviet Union that the color pictures were faked. An American businessman had attempted to bring in two hundred copies of the magazine to be given to people he met in Russia, but the magazines were confiscated with that excuse.

ARIZONA PEOPLE

On a headstone in Arlington National Cemetery is the inscription:

William O. O'Neill
Mayor of Prescott, Arizona
Captain, Troop A, First U.S.
Volunteer Cavalry, Rough Riders
Brevet Major
Born Feb. 2, 1860. Killed July 1, 1898
At San Juan Hill, Cuba
"Who Would Not Die for a New Star on the Flag?"

The stirring saga of "Buckey" O'Neill symbolized the adventuresome spirit of people who settled in Arizona Territory in the closing decades of the nineteenth century. This handsome young Irishman was court reporter, newspaper editor and publisher, Republican office-seeker in a Democratic stronghold, and lover of life. His nickname was not acquired during his brief service as a Rough Rider under Teddy Roosevelt, but for his daring at faro, where he delighted in "bucking the tiger" with his last gold piece.

Yet this love of gambling did not prevent him from serving with courage and distinction as Sheriff of huge Yavapai County, when he tracked train robbers through the snow far into Utah and brought them to justice. Like nearly all Arizonans he came here from elsewhere, in this case, St. Louis, but his short life in this rough and wild territory left a mark that will long be remembered. The monument to the Rough Riders, a cavalry officer brandishing his saber from his rearing mount, bears a face that resembles no one member of the Arizona contingent that stormed San Juan Hill that hot July day. But all those who see it in front of the Yavapai County court house at Prescott *know* they are seeing Buckey O'Neill. It is his type that transformed Arizona from a land of lawless terror into a civilized state.

*   *   *

If Buckey O'Neill wandered far from his lawful jurisdiction in tracking train robbers into Utah, another Arizona sheriff outdid him by going into Mexico to arrest his quarry. Carl Hayden was Sheriff of Maricopa County before going to Washington, D.C. in 1912 as the state's first Congressman. His policy of speaking seldom and then softly worked so well that he went on to pile up more than a half century of service in the Congress of the United States before retirement in 1968. As longtime Chairman of the Senate Appropriations Committee and President Pro Tem of the Senate, Carl Hayden became one of the most powerful and respected leaders of our nation, serving under ten Presidents. After retirement Senator Hayden worked on his papers in the offices of the gleaming new library bearing his name, on the Tempe campus of Arizona State University. He was the first white child to be born in that town, and, as a native son, was a member of one of Arizona's most vocal minorities. When he passed away peacefully in his sleep in 1972, aged ninety-four, America lost a great and true friend.

*   *   *

Arizona's greats have made their places in history at various periods of maturity. Buckey O'Neill had lived a rich and vigorous life as a newspaperman, sheriff and judge when cut down at San Juan Hill at age thirty-eight. Carl Hayden won his spurs at law enforcement in his thirties, and went on to represent his state in the halls of Congress for more than a half century after that. But Frank Luke, Jr. perished at only twenty-one, following thirty-nine days of fame on the Western Front in France during the fall of 1918, to be forever listed among the real heroes of Arizona, as the 27th Aero Squadron's famed "Balloon Buster."

A maverick who disdained military discipline and took off on his own whenever possible, young Luke was the terror of his sector, with twenty-one victories in his short fighting career. His final patrol on September 29 was a fitting climax to that saga of the skies. After shooting down three German observation balloons, which were always heavily protected and considered more dangerous targets than enemy aircraft, he was wounded and crash landed near the village of Murvaux, strafing German troops as he landed. When called upon to surrender he drew his pistol and continued to fire until killed. Pilots who now train at Luke Air Force Base near Phoenix visit the State Capitol to view his statue in front of the building. Imbedded in the base is a replica of one of the first Congressional Medals of Honor awarded an aviator, based upon those events of September 29, 1918. His was a spirit much like that of Buckey O'Neill, of whom it was said "He Stayed With 'Em While He Lasted."

*   *   *

Del Webb came to Arizona in 1929 to work as a carpenter, after a sporadic career as a minor league baseball pitcher in California. In less than twenty years he was head of a mammoth construction firm engaged in building projects in all parts of the United States and was half owner of the New York Yankees. His great experiment in new community planning started in 1960, when the first Sun City was begun on flat farmlands a few miles northwest of Phoenix.

Little more than a decade later, Sun City, Arizona boasted an enthusiastic population of nearly 20,000, and was joined by other Sun Cities in California and Florida. Full-fledged retirement communities, the Sun Cities require that at least one resident of each home be fifty or older, resulting in an average age in the sixties. Those "senior citizens" are on the go constantly, choosing from a bewildering assortment of activities and clubs. Del Webb treats them to entertainment in the Sun Bowl from time to time, and his choice is more likely to be his old friends Guy Lombardo or Lawrence Welk rather than rock groups. But he's giving his residents what they and he like. Although Del Webb's name is on the Big Board of the New York Stock Exchange now, his headquarters remain loyally and firmly planted in Phoenix.

*　　　*　　　*

"Barry Was Right" proclaims a large banner on the side of a curio store north of Scottsdale on the Carefree highway. There are a lot of folks out Arizona way who think this way, even though the American electorate didn't agree in 1964. Barry Goldwater is probably the best known Arizonan today, and carries on the image of this frontier land as a man who talks straight and says plainly what he thinks.

Barry's roots in Arizona go back quite a way, to Grandfather Michael's first store at Ehrenberg, Arizona in 1862. This village on the Colorado River soon lost its luster as a major shipping port for river steamers and Goldwater stores were established at Phoenix and Prescott in 1872 and 1879. Barry's uncle Morris ran the Prescott operation, and set some kind of a record for longevity as Mayor of that city, serving twenty years over a forty-eight year period. In memory of Uncle Morris Barry traditionally launches each of his political campaigns in front of the Rough Rider statue at Prescott.

Barry's start in politics was influenced by his interest in photography, particularly of Arizona's Indian tribes. Slide shows given to civic groups around the state in the 1940s, combined with his publication in *Arizona Highways*, made his name a familiar one throughout the state. Now back in the United States Senate, he is away from Arizona more than he would prefer, but his Phoenix hilltop home is constantly alive with activity, reflecting Barry's second hobby as a radio "ham." A crew of radio operators is on duty each day to man Barry's station, relaying calls from servicemen in foreign lands to their families in this country via "patched" telephone lines.

*　　　*　　　*

One of the Arizona women who left their mark on this land, Lulu R. Hall, owned and operated hotels in northern Arizona after being forced to flee from Mexico during the revolution of 1914. Her Beale Hotel's letterheads in Kingman always bore the notation "L. R. Hall, Proprietor." This might have meant she felt it was still a man's world in those days, and that "Mrs." might somehow lessen the effectiveness of business operations. She seemed to be amused that letters sent in response to those written on such letterheads were invariably addressed to "Mr. L. R. Hall." She had purchased the Beale

Hotel from the parents of gravel-voiced movie star Andy Devine, and it was the Ritz and the Waldorf of northwestern Arizona in its day. Most guests walked across the street from the Santa Fe train depot, but an ever-increasing number checked in from dust-covered automobiles that had somehow traversed the bumpy miles of US 66. The faded register of the Beale has recorded some famous names—Greta Garbo, Clark Gable, and that era's foremost hero, Charles A. Lindbergh, who gave a quarter tip to a boy who brought a telegram to his room. I still have that quarter as a treasured memento of the happy and exciting days spent amid the corridors and rooms of Grandmother Hall's Beale Hotel.

*   *   *

If these six Arizonans indeed represent the people who have chosen to make this state their home, it would seem that the salient characteristic they shared was independence. Each stood on his own feet and did his own thing. Two of them are still doing it as honored citizens of our own time. They typify today's Arizonan, who finds his own way and sets his own pace to a degree not found elsewhere in this land, except perhaps in our newest frontier state of Alaska.

The stock broker who walks among the skyscrapers of Central Avenue in Phoenix may appear identical to his counterpart on Wall Street, but the Arizonan knows that he has a far different way of life close at hand when the day's work is done. So, too, it is with other office workers and the electronics technicians assembling transistors and integrated circuits. Their functions and work surroundings could be placed in Chicago or Los Angeles, but their world outside the factory walls could not!

Most of them are newcomers, but they have quickly assumed roles of leading activity in all aspects of community life. The "Old Guard" of native sons and daughters, or even those who arrived here just before the days of World War II are thoroughly outnumbered and do not wield the influence that their contemporaries might back in, say, Ohio or Alabama: most of the parents of civic, business, and social leaders weren't native Arizonans. One might think that California would be pretty much the same way, but there is a stronger thread of continuity over there in the Golden State: a much stronger and larger group of natives whose roots go back several generations, including more than a hundred years of University of California graduates. As they were graduating, residents of Arizona Territory were kept busy in an attempt to stay alive in the land of Geronimo, the Apache chief. The only winter visitors in those days were in transit from the civilized East to fairly well civilized California, and they got through Arizona as quickly as possible, welcoming the protection of the United States Army and the colorful Arizona Rangers.

Arizonans, newcomers to a desert land, are glad to be part of a new life, simple and informal at home, and delight in getting full enjoyment of the vast and colorful land that surrounds them. People on the go, they can use Arizona's great variety of elevations and climatic zones to pick and choose from among several seasons of the year on any given day. Just now becoming aware that this great outdoors which they enjoy so thoroughly is a somewhat fragile item, they are also a concerned people. Most have moved to Arizona to seek the Better Life, and the thought of somehow losing it disturbs them: where could they go from here?

The Future

Rich in natural beauty and peopled largely by a band of young newcomers enthused by the prospect of making a new start on the semi-frontier, Arizona's direction seems to be upward to bigger things. But Town Hall, a gathering of some hundred prominent citizens that spends three days each year discussing a subject of importance to the state's future, thought otherwise. 1970's topic was "Man's Relationship to his Environment," and the group, somewhat "establishment" in orientation, came up with a recommendation that made headlines from Page on the Utah border to Nogales right next door to Sonora, Mexico.

The "Man Bites Dog" angle was that they felt Arizona should no longer encourage more industry and more people to come into this state, that we have enough of both right now: our energy should be towards the goal of "Better, Not Bigger."

The approach isn't entirely original. In recent years there has been a fellow in Washington state vigorously advocating something called "Lesser Seattle." The idea was picked up and warmly supported by a columnist for the *Los Angeles Times*, although that gentleman observed it was probably too late to save the City of Angels from *its* plight.

For Arizona, the idea was revolutionary—for days afterwards the favorite question was, "Do they really mean it?" The moment of truth may arrive when a petition is brought to the Phoenix City Council for rezoning so the XYZ Widgit Company can build a new factory that will bring in two thousand additional jobs. But how can we prevent or even discourage people from picking up stakes and moving to Arizona, as many of those attending that Town Hall at the Grand Canyon did in recent years? California tried that during Dust

20

Bowl days, and it is not one of the prouder chapters in our neighbor's long history.

The question is thorny, but the major thrust of the Town Hall statement leads us to think seriously about Arizona's future development. We have seen what Arizona seems to be today, how it got there, and now we should take a look at where it goes from here.

I

TOWN HALL felt that the aim should be for quality, keeping the numbers where they are. But since Arizona's growth is not likely to taper off, it would seem best to anticipate the inevitable, and direct it into useful channels. Complete new cities have been carefully planned in every detail before the first bulldozer began to turn ground. One such city on Arizona's border, Boulder City, Nevada, was created at the completion of Hoover Dam. The federal government did the planning and much of the building for this pleasant oasis in the desert.

Within Arizona there are examples of complete city planning performed within the private sector, previews of things to come. Except for mining camps which were company towns, the oldest example is Litchfield Park, just west of Phoenix. It is a development of Goodyear Tire and Rubber Company, whose chief executive, Paul Litchfield, grew interested in this part of the Salt River Valley as a source of long-staple cotton for use in tire bodies. The town was laid out around a square bordering on the grounds of the Wigwam, a luxury winter resort, one of Arizona's first refuges for those fleeing the Midwest's blizzards. The town itself managed to carry on for several decades but is now being vastly expanded as a "bedroom community" for Phoenix.

Within commuting distance of Phoenix, Litchfield Park is generally considered a suburban development, even though a thoroughly planned one. Quite different is the concept of Del Webb's Sun City, just a few miles north. In this community, which started from nothing in the midst of bean fields, only persons over fifty may purchase homes or apartments, and children may not reside in the town. Sun City people tend to stay pretty much at home, where they participate in endless civic and personal projects, and only a small number commute to other communities in the valley to continue working. A retirement community, its residents have come from all parts of the United States to begin new lives among contemporaries.

An exciting new city has sprung up in the desert far from any center of population, and seems the best model for the future. This example of planned

21

city "imagineering" is called Lake Havasu City, after the huge man-made body of water formed by damming the Colorado River.

In just ten years the barren desert has been transformed into a bustling, modern city of 10,000 exactly on schedule towards its planned goal of 75,000 residents. The success of Lake Havasu City is due to a policy of flying prospective residents from all parts of the United States, in contrast to "buy land by mail" schemes that have plagued Arizona in recent years. The other reason is that the city rests squarely on a solid foundation of industrial payrolls. The result is a population quite like most American towns of similar size: not a retirement or recreation community, but planned as a normal city with a normal distribution of age groups.

Lake Havasu City probably could have continued on its orderly schedule of development and growth with only its scenic charm, availability of water sports, and care in civic planning to recommend it, but in 1968 came the announcement that it would become Arizona's home for the London Bridge, news that made front pages around the world. London's Lord Mayor laid the bridge's new cornerstone with much pomp and pageantry in September of that year. Work began of transporting the historic stones across the ocean to the Arizona desert. Dedicated in 1971, it already rivals the Grand Canyon as Arizona's number one visitor attraction.

North of Nogales, near the Mexican border, another planned city of a similar type is developing, and bringing prospective residents to the site before they purchase land. Rio Rico lies on high, rolling grasslands like those in the motion picture version of *Oklahoma!* which was filmed not far from this spot. The estimated final population is also 75,000.

Near Phoenix are two more complete planned city developments. The smaller, a 4,000-acre community, is set on a Scottsdale ranch once owned by the McCormick family, of International Harvester. The giant Kaiser-Aetna corporation is developing it as one of a series of new cities they have built in California and Hawaii. East of the McCormick Ranch is Fountain Hills, planned for 60,000 inhabitants, another development of the McCulloch Corporation which built Lake Havasu City. For its centerpiece it has a five hundred foot jet of water patterned after Geneva's *Jet d'Eau*.

II

Even if Litchfield Park, Sun City, Rio Rico, Lake Havasu City and Fountain Hills all continue their carefully charted paths it will not be enough to alleviate Arizona's growing pains. Many more will be required, and the smaller communities which did not share in the dizzy growth of the past three decades will probably become major city developments. "How you goin' to keep them down on the farm after they've seen Paree?" went the 1918 song. And how you goin' to shunt Arizona newcomers away from Phoenix and Tucson into the fresh air of the hinterlands?

Rapid transit systems could be developed permitting residents of new satellite communities fifty to seventy miles away to commute easily to jobs in the big city centers: the expansion of Arizona's freeway system would encourage developments around Phoenix and Tucson. Or, enough worthwhile jobs could be provided in the new cities, to bring and keep people there. But even in a new city as far as sixty miles from downtown Phoenix, the big-city features of shopping and entertainment would still be but an hour away.

Smaller communities much farther away will still come to view Phoenix and Tucson as pleasant and convenient one-day destinations on the network of superhighways that is quickly bringing Arizona together again. Major terrain barriers like the Black Canyon north of Phoenix and the Salt River Gorge, Arizona's "Little Grand Canyon," have yielded to the skill of the road builders, so that Flagstaff and Show Low residents can plan quick and easy visits to the big city.

III

ONE PLANNER of new cities has decided to build one of his own, using his own hands and those of his students. Paolo Soleri came to Arizona from his native Italy to study under Frank Lloyd Wright. He has since developed his own distinctive style for soaring architecture, viewing the entire city as a subject. His first city of the future, now under construction in the brushy highlands about eighty miles north of Phoenix, serves as an example and inspiration for others who seek a new form of life in the western desert.

Soleri's "mound houses" attracted worldwide attention, and are typical of the free forms of artistic statement that seem to flourish in this state. Best known in architecture was his great teacher Frank Lloyd Wright, whose Taliesen West settlement in the foothills of the McDowell Mountains northeast of Scottsdale now serves as headquarters for his followers. Arizona was Wright's winter home and workplace, and the state has had the benefit of many of his structures, the most notable being a majestic concert hall at Arizona State University in Tempe. Not far away is the state's finest example of Mexican-influenced architecture in the new Scottsdale City Hall and Library complex by Bennie Gonzalez.

Yet with all these examples of inspired design, it is remarkable that the bulk of homes and other buildings here could have been designed for Connecticut or Iowa! Phoenix is a far worse offender than Tucson, for the latter has a much stronger Mexican influence in its architecture, and many of the results are very pleasant. Such buildings should be placed on a lot of respectable size, and the rolling foothills of Tucson's Santa Catalina Mountains contain many such "mini-estates" of about one acre. Acre lots are the rule in most of the area northeast of Phoenix as well, but here the houses seem to resemble an Arizona builder's idea of a Cape Cod cottage or Wisconsin farmhouse. Even a horse or two in the backyard corral doesn't seem to help establish a western flavor.

But, it's what sells. When Frank Lloyd Wright agreed to design a modest "cottage" for Raymond Carlson, Carlson had a difficult time securing financing in Phoenix. The Wright design was too "controversial" then, but that home will retain its charm and integrity long after its neighbors have been razed and forgotten.

I V

PAINTERS, TOO, have trouble establishing their own styles. Tucson's Ted de Grazia was a "starving artist" when *Arizona Highways* first publicized him. He had accepted a position on the Mexican border as a cattle inspector when his first fame came. "Raymond Carlson saved me from hoof and mouth disease," Ted informs visitors to his sprawling adobe gallery in the Santa Catalina foothills. He has become so successful that he feels he can no longer afford to sell his paintings. As he does new work, usually in series, like his pictorial history of Father Kino's travels through Arizona in the seventeenth century, he has it reproduced in book and print forms, keeping the original oils and watercolors for himself.

Notable art groups have sprung up, particularly in Scottsdale, Sedona, Tucson and Tubac. These are year-round locations, while Flagstaff is mainly a summer art center. Scottsdale even has a stained glass studio supplying windows for churches and office buildings throughout the nation. More than a dozen art galleries are busy throughout the year, with a half dozen added for the winter visitor season. The red rocks of Oak Creek Canyon provide daily inspiration for the Sedona group, who don't care that James Swinnerton, the West's foremost painter, said that Sedona folks get mad at each other because they're always seeing red! Jimmy is still Number One painter out in these parts, but he's only an amateur psychologist. The future of art in Arizona looks very bright, for artists flourish in direct proportion to the number of customers they attract, which is constantly increasing. Few tourists depart Arizona without a de Grazia or two, even if they are only prints or reproductions on note cards. The soft woven fabrics of Scottsdale's Lloyd Kiva or the brilliantly colored plastic shapes of his young neighbor, Dick Seeger, are distinctively Arizonian, as are the melodic wind bells cast by Paolo Soleri to provide a source of cash income while his grand new cities take shape.

Traditional Arizona handicrafts are the silver and turquoise objects fashioned by Indians, particularly the Hopi and Navajo peoples. They have unique beauty and charm, but reflect the problems that face all tribal Arizonans. The profit margin of Indian craftsmen is pitifully thin, and does little to remove the grinding poverty that afflicts the reservations.

Massive introduction of industrial work has already started in neighboring New Mexico, and the electronics manufacturers find that hands which patiently fashion stands of silver can also be trained to assemble semi-conductors and integrated circuits. But Indians form ten percent of the state's population—there's so much to be done.

As industry does move slowly in establishing new factories in or near the Indian reservations, some tribes have taken advantage of the scenic and recreational assets their lands possess. The White Mountain Apache ski resort, camping parks and motels in eastern Arizona's high country, and creation of new man-made fishing lakes on the vast expanse of Navajo reservations show the Indians are anxious to help themselves to a higher standard of living, and are capable workers in the administration of such developments. We hope Arizona's Indians find their rightful share in their state's growth.

V

As ARIZONA's network of Interstate Highways continues to be filled in, these new recreational areas in far-flung corners of the state will become increasingly more convenient to visitors from the big cities. Arizona is unique in having three large segments of the nation's Interstate system that will both cut down travel time and open up new scenic vistas.

The "Brenda Cutoff" brings Phoenix nearly an hour closer to Los Angeles on Interstate Highway 10. The earlier routing headed far northward to the dude ranch town of Wickenburg—following the centuries-old pattern of wagon travel. The new road heads due west from Phoenix through the Harquahala Valley, site of huge mechanized farming operations, including some of the nation's largest commercial rose gardens. The good folks of Wickenburg weren't very happy about being bypassed, but growing traffic between Phoenix and Las Vegas will help cheer them up.

Up north, in Mohave and Yavapai Counties, the successor to famed

US 66 ("Get Your Kicks on Route 66") will head east of Kingman as Interstate Highway 40, also traveling through rugged mountain country en route to Seligman. The routing that it replaces and shortens by forty miles is a historic one pioneered by Lt. Edward Fitzgerald Beale, U.S.N., in 1857, with his camel train. His trail was later used as a route for the Santa Fe Railroad and US 66 followed that as a sort of line of least resistance. Now the modern highway makers will strike out anew, using the magic of stereoscopic aerial photo interpretation to find the most feasible line for new ribbons of travel.

The most spectacular new highway routing in Arizona is more a part of Utah and Nevada than Arizona. Interstate Highway 15 slices through the extreme northwestern corner of Arizona as it leads from Las Vegas to St. George, Utah. Engineers determined that the best and most direct route would lead through the gorge of the Virgin River in what is turning out to be the most expensive bit of highway building in the entire Interstate system. For about two million dollars a mile a fantastic roadway is being cut through this canyon, a scenic extravaganza that will be worth a trip in its own right. Arizona, which derives zero benefit from this road, is stuck with the tab through a quirk of geography.

These three freeways are but a part of the nationwide network of fast, safe and comfortable superhighways that will bring exciting new opportunities for vacation trips for more of our citizens. When completed, the Interstate system will bring Arizona within range of New York or Florida for two-week vacations by car, a full week in Arizona for only seven days round trip. And recent experiments in summer promotion by Phoenix and Tucson luxury resorts have sparked a keen interest in their bargain rates, with refrigerated air conditioning tempering the summer heat.

The freeways will bring all parts of this huge state within easy reach of its two main population centers for one-day shopping or entertainment trips, permit the establishment of complete new cities as big-city commuting suburbs as far as seventy miles away, and bring Arizona within reach of the two-week vacation travelers driving from any part of the United States. This is quite another ball game!

VI

As ARIZONA attempts to solve its water problem in the central valley by importing water from Lake Havasu through Central Arizona Project's aqueducts and tunnels, another large man-made desert lake will be formed by Orme Dam on the Verde River east of Scottsdale. It will be another major water sports area, the closest to Phoenix and right at the doorstep of developing Fountain Hills. This new lake will also benefit the Indians of the Fort McDowell Reservation, who will be able to build marinas and picnic areas on lakefront land.

This new lake behind Orme Dam will follow the example of others on the Salt and Verde Rivers, lakes whose primary purpose is water storage for irrigation, but which also offer fishing, boating and water ski areas less than an hour from downtown Phoenix.

The future of agriculture in the Valley of the Sun around Phoenix is uncertain, even if badly needed Lake Havasu waters are delivered through the Central Arizona Project in the 1970s. As water tables continue to drop through constant pumping to supplement waters delivered from the Salt River reservoirs, many farmers find pumping costs exceed the value of crops produced. Then crop lands revert to their former desert condition. The huge influx of new residents has not aggravated the water problem: in fact as crop lands are converted to housing tracts, the water use drops tremendously from that required for crop irrigation. Though there is plenty of water in sight for people in Arizona, today's rich harvest of agricultural products may be in its last stage. With just so much water to go around, the people's needs may have to take precedence over farming.

VII

IN THE future, visitor promotion and the subsequent care and feeding of those visitors who heed the call will contribute greatly to the economy. New hotels and resorts spring up yearly and jumbo jets bring in people to fill them up. Some will decide to stay, and they will need schools and myriad services in the state's various communities. As visitors, though, they make few demands on the usual facilities of our cities. The state is a big one, and countless new areas remain to be developed for enjoyment by the golfers, fishermen and sportsmen attracted to Arizona by *Arizona Highways* and stories told by friends about the pleasures of this state.

Many are just learning of the year round joys of life in the pine forests of northern and eastern Arizona, covering half the state. Hundreds of summer cottages at Pinetop and Flagstaff house Phoenix families whose breadwinners commute from Phoenix, and many of the state's newest 18-hole golf courses have been constructed in the high country. It would be hard to make a dent in the tremendous expanse of forest land, and the desert fishing lakes like Havasu or Mohave are dramatic contrasts to heavily congested California lakes with their "wall to wall boats." The fisherman on Lake Mohave who feels hemmed in when another boat is in sight can just chug downlake a ways and take over a few more square miles of water.

VIII

THE FORESTS and lakes and broad deserts are all out there for the leisure of Arizonans and visitors. The tourist industry is important, but those who put down roots in this state must rely on steady jobs. New and interesting work will be needed to sustain additional residents.

The meteoric rise of the electronics industry following World War II has been mentioned, and this growth will most likely continue. Workers here seem more productive and contented, and less subject to absenteeism in the Phoenix and Tucson semiconductor plants than their counterparts back east.

In the service field, the product is paperwork: an exciting example is the American Express credit card headquarters in Phoenix. Its world-wide affiliates funnel work into this central point: processing and billing is done with the latest and most sophisticated computing equipment. Since this type of operation could be located anywhere, American Express' choice of Arizona shows it feels the residents of this state are good workers.

Convention travel is encouraged by improved highways and air schedules into Phoenix and Tucson, and the major resort hotels have constructed impressive meeting facilities, supplementing immense new convention centers in Tucson and Phoenix.

The three state universities at Tucson, Tempe and Flagstaff continue to add to their stature. A fourth university on the west side of Phoenix may someday balance the enrollment of Arizona State at Tempe on the eastern edge of the capital. New junior colleges like Central Arizona College some forty miles south of Phoenix, dot the state. Two thousand students attend this one, located in the barren desert more than twenty miles from the distractions of any city or town.

Arizona State at Tempe, already known as a computer-oriented campus, will enlarge its close associations with firms in Phoenix and Scottsdale such as the Honeywell plant in Phoenix, that manufacture electronics components, including full lines of high-powered electronic computers. And at Tucson, the University of Arizona will build on its reputation for leadership in astronomy, with its large and complete optical laboratories on campus supporting Kitt Peak National Observatory's work eighty miles west.

Kitt Peak is the site of the world's largest solar telescope, which can spot solar flares that might endanger flights into outer space. The new facilities at Tucson will carry on in astronomy, as does Lowell Observatory in Flagstaff, where the planet Pluto was discovered in the 1930s. Space-associated studies will continue at Flagstaff as additional moon-mapping is done by the U.S. Aeronautical and Charting Service and lunar geology is studied by the Flagstaff laboratories of the U.S. Geological Survey. Most of America's astronauts are familiar visitors to the Arizona scene as they use the state's volcanic crater fields for moon simulations.

IX

IN ITS "cow country" days, much of Arizona's state business was conducted on a very informal basis in the lobby of the Adams Hotel in downtown Phoenix when the State Legislature was in session, but in the 1970s Arizona is acquiring new maturity in governmental and social responsibilities. As Governor Jack Williams took the oath of office for another term in January 1971, he was starting the first four-year term of office in that post. As a long-time radio commentator with a keen interest in Arizona history and progress, the Governor ably expressed the state's opportunities and goals:

"We have been living on the dreams and success of men who came out here to build the homes, the ranches, to develop the mines and create industry.

"They came because they were intrigued with the open space, what we call our way of life, the natural beauties and wonders of Arizona. And they brought with them civilization which included clutter, crowded conditions, and in some instances, an increase in pollution.

"These people left us with homes, water, electricity, a pretty good highway system—a far better place than they found it.

"Now we have no more right to deny others to come here than those who lived here at the beginning had a right to deny us.

"But the big question of the 70s is what we are going to do for our posterity. What are we going to leave for those who come after?

"I believe we can take industry, create green belts and disperse industry throughout the state so there are enough jobs available and yet we remain selective.

"We must plan for garden-type industry, well landscaped, well scattered with lots of green space. Perhaps we'll have to get away from grid block development and begin growing vertically instead of laterally.

"In short, we must reorient our goals and begin to determine what kind of state we want this to be."

Governor Williams knows that he will be aided by a more skilled and professional corps of governmental assistants. When the reins of government were still held by natives who had grown up on its soil, Arizona did not give up its image as a frontier state. But the state's "garden" industries in the 1950s and 1960s brought a new and different breed of citizen, highly skilled and educated people who would run complex technical operations.

Most moved to the Arizona desert for reasons other than financial gain, and some took substantial pay cuts. As these managers and engineers have assumed their new roles as Arizonans they have enriched many aspects of community and state life, including government work. And they attract others of like caliber. In return they acquire the informal and low-pressure characteristics of this land. They do not just do business as in New York or Chicago. The promise of Arizona is the best of the two worlds.

The managers and government leaders the newcomers replaced were fine people who did business in a friendly and honorable manner, but most of those from the cow country days realize and acknowledge that today's society demands a high degree of technical skill and expertise. When the "One Man— One Vote" principle was applied to this state many senior legislators of outstanding character were involuntarily retired from public life. But the resulting makeup of the State Legislature is a much more representative one.

The World War II fliers who came back in the late 1940s began a tremendous surge, but the opportunities are present today as they were in 1946. To help in the task of shaping a future Arizona, people have come here, many at bargain rates, to make new starts in life. They see great opportunity in a land that is new and still largely undeveloped: a land where their talents and willingness to work hard will bring rich rewards in satisfaction and contentment.

This is the dream that brought Michael Goldwater to the banks of the muddy Colorado to found a mercantile establishment at Ehrenberg, Arizona in 1862, the lure that Buckey O'Neill followed west from St. Louis in 1879 and Del Webb pursued a half century later, a dream that would have been spread by word of mouth if there had never been an *Arizona Highways* magazine and a young man named Carlson to make it flourish, but the dream developed more fully and more quickly because of them. The frontier is still there for men and women of purpose—the doers of our land, and that frontier's name is Arizona.

"A HECK OF A PLACE TO LOSE A COW"

So went the comment of an Arizona cowhand when asked for his first reaction to this view. It ranks with the one attributed to Teddy Roosevelt, "Golly—what a gulley!"

The spot is Mohave Point on the West Rim Drive skirting the Grand Canyon's edge from Bright Angel Lodge to Hermit's Rest. Each turnout gives a different aspect of this subject which also seems to change in color, texture and mood with the passage of just five minutes spent driving between lookout points.

Less tranquil is the scene left behind at Bright Angel Lodge, where batallions of the Fred Harvey organization wage a game but losing battle each summer in attempting to feed and house the torrents of visitors who besiege this small strip of land bordering the chasm. Much more pleasant is an off-season trip to the Grand Canyon, when the majesty of this scene is best enjoyed amid conditions of tranquility.

The summer of 1973 marked the beginning of an experiment in free transportation of visitors along the West Rim Drive by park minibus in an effort to reduce automobile congestion. The results are not yet in, but some complications might be expected from those tourists reluctant to be dragged away from the edge when just on the verge of taking *the* definitive picture of the Grand Canyon. The Canyon is a tough subject, and most visitors would be well advised to stock up on postcards and picture books to back up their own efforts.

32

TERROR AT TOROWEAP

While many visitors to Grand Canyon Village on the South Rim use words such as "awesome" and "terrifying" on picture postcards sent back home, the terms are not to be taken literally, at least as to actual danger. Not so here at Toroweap Point, where that first wrong step is a straight drop several thousand feet right into the muddy Colorado River. This is where the Canyon is very narrow and very deep, a spot reached only after some difficulty over narrow and dusty roads entirely devoid of service stations, hamburger stands, or even guideposts. Toroweap is truly both an awesome and terrifying experience for the few hundred adventuresome souls who find it each year. But it is well worth the quest.

Those who grumble over the inconvenience of travel to Toroweap to take a few quick snapshots of the gorge might reflect for a moment on the methods used by one J. K. Hillers in the year 1872. Hillers avoided the dust of travel over the untouched expanse of the vast plateau by the simple expedient of reaching this point in a frail wooden boat as a member of the second Powell expedition. All that remained to be done was to scale the almost vertical cliff carrying heavy camera, tripod, glass plates and darkroom tent in which to coat the plates and to subsequently develop them while still damp from initial coating. The result? Equal or superior to our best efforts today, a rather humbling experience to a present-day photographer who may think he's pretty good at his trade.

34

SPRINGTIME COMES TO OAK CREEK CANYON

The color of springtime merely adds to the year 'round splendor of this charming spot south of Flagstaff. The lush valley floor and dramatic canyon walls have made Oak Creek Canyon a favorite vacation place for Arizona residents since the turn of the century, when Theodore Carlton Schnebly constructed an access road to scale the sheer walls. That road, still unpaved, leads from the canyon's only town, Sedona, up Schnebly Hill to the pine-covered heights of the plateau. This area has long been a favorite setting for "shoot-'em-up" western movie making, a sight that delighted my grandmother, Lulu Hall, when she occupied a home overlooking the rocks wherein the dramas were played out. Now in and around Sedona retired people who had built modest cottages on the red dirt in an effort to get away from it all are faced with a minor population explosion.

36

TREES TURNED TO STONE

Petrified Forest National Park, near Holbrook, is a unique preserve for the care and protection of trees that became colorful stone in ages past. The Park's location astride busy Interstate Highway 40 makes it one of America's most heavily visited, which creates a problem that is also unique. The sheer size and weight of the big logs seem to assure them a continuing place in this display, but the pocket-sized bits and pieces turn out to be the stakes in a grim struggle waged between Park Rangers and The Great American Touring Public. Since the rangers seem to be hopelessly outnumbered in this bout, we can but applaud their dedication to duty and hope for the best. While perhaps of small consolation, the present situation must be considered some improvement over that obtaining prior to establishment of the area as a National Monument in 1906. Before that entire trainloads of petrified logs were hauled away for commercial use. Public indignation finally demanded action when one firm began to crush logs to obtain material for the manufacture of abrasive grinding wheels!

MONTEZUMA NEVER SLEPT HERE

Early Arizona settlers sometimes took liberties in applying place names. Montezuma Castle National Monument is an example. The Aztec chieftain met his end in 1519 in what is now downtown Mexico City and most certainly never saw this part of central Arizona. The builders of this fine five-story structure first settled the area in the eleventh century, A.D., and had left most of their dwellings in this Verde Valley region by the beginning of the fifteenth century.

I well remember visiting here in my youth, when a series of ladders permitted tourists to clamber up into the rooms. The ladders have long since been removed, and present-day travelers make the one-mile detour from Interstate 17 merely to observe from the valley floor. This was an early favorite photographic subject of *Arizona Highways* photographer Ray Manley, who grew up in nearby Cottonwood. He worked diligently to improve "the field of fire" by cutting off many dead tree limbs, thus providing a vastly improved view of the Castle for future generations of shutter clickers.

VALLEY OF THE MONUMENTS

John Ford first convinced the American public that a place such as Monument Valley could be real when he gave us the classic film, *Stagecoach*, in 1939. Yet despite all of the publicity given by this and many other Ford films and numerous issues of *Arizona Highways* magazine, the roughest roads in the West kept tourists out of this mysterious region on the Utah–Arizona border until pavement came in the early 1960s.

This is one of the major dwelling places of the Navajo Indians, and life in the hogan at Monument Valley is likely to be much as it was in the days of *Stagecoach* filming. Harry Goulding still runs the trading post and offers rooms for the night. The latter enterprise started when John Ford needed an instant tent city to house his actors and crew. It's far from the beaten track, but that view from Goulding's at sunset won't be found anywhere else on this planet.

ROCKS THAT STAND LIKE MEN

The strange rock formations in Chiricahua National Monument, tucked away in Arizona's southeastern corner, are the result of massive lava flows, earth uplifts and tiltings, earthquakes and erosion. This was the home of the Chiricahua Apaches, one of the most savage and warlike tribes in American history, finally rounded up and shipped to Florida in 1882 to permanently remove their menace from the Arizona scene. A walking trail leads from Massai Point through a wonderland of balanced rocks which require only a slight amount of imagination to recognize as Donald Duck, Baked Potato, Punch & Judy and the Organ Pipes. As a lofty mountain range set in a desert sea, the Chiricahuas have developed their own animal and plant varieties. This led to establishment of a major research station by the American Museum of Natural History on the eastern slope of the Chiricahua Mountains, reached by a highly scenic back road trip from the Monument. The only thing left unresolved about this historic land of Cochise and Geronimo is pronunciation of the name—the early settlers of the area just called it the "Cheery Cows" and let it go at that.

SAIL ON . . . SAIL ON!

Many towns in the East are proud of rock formations on nearby hills that seem to look like human heads or other objects. It is usually a bit difficult to puzzle them out, but there is no doubt about this famed landmark west of Fredonia on the road to Pipe Spring National Monument. Anyone who doesn't agree that we have here a majestic ocean liner steaming through a billowing sea goes to the foot of the class. It's sometimes called Ship Rock, but this gets confused with the well-known rock of that name north of Gallup, New Mexico, which resembles a ship of an earlier era with all sails set. Battleship Rock is another name for this pride of northern Arizona's Mohave County, but I prefer just plain old Steamboat Rock. It's a fine, big ship, indeed, measuring about 1,000 feet in length, or just about the length of a major passenger liner or an aircraft carrier, which this rock resembles to a startling degree. It's a prized feature of the "Strip Country" of Arizona, a barren and deserted portion of the state cut off from the rest of Arizona by that great roadblock, the Grand Canyon of the Colorado.

46

THE PEAKS

A more precise and authoritative title for the Alp-like mountains shown here near Flagstaff would be the San Francisco Peaks, topped by 12,670-foot Humphreys Peak, Arizona's highest point. But to residents of northern Arizona, from California to New Mexico borders, a mere reference to "The Peaks" will suffice—everyone will know the mountains you have in mind. The snow waters starting their merry way to Arizona's desert lowlands are one important source of the state's supply of precious water for both agriculture and urban living needs. These rivulets and brooks will eventually reach the Verde River and its series of reservoirs. Heavier accumulations of snow in the White and Blue Mountains near the New Mexico border will melt off and flow into the Salt and Gila Rivers.

Meanwhile, as a winter bonus, the slopes of the Arizona Ski Bowl are alive with activity on that portion of the mountain sloping out of the picture on the left. These mountains form an impressive backdrop to Flagstaff, one of the state's most active and energetic cities, whose interests run the gamut from studies of the ancient past at the Musuem of Northern Arizona to far-out investigations of new and better ways to transport Man across the surface of the Moon! Higher education and scientific research flourish here at 7,000 feet amid the pines.

48

THE DESERT CLOUDBURST

Summer rains sometimes add to the water supply stored in lakes behind Arizona's great dams, but more frequently a sand wash such as this one near Yucca in Mohave County will simply dry up and disappear before it reaches any major running river. Yet, the sight of a running wash during a cloudburst is always a great thrill, bringing back many memories of washes closing major transcontinental highways in the days prior to adequate bridging. The most vivid memory of a scene such as this, however, is not a visual one at all, but rather the unique smell of wet greasewood, sage brush, and mesquite which pervades the air. At times this distinctive odor is carried by the wind long before a storm reaches an area—it is an unmistakable sign that welcome rain is on the way. It is the mark of a true desert rat that he will stand at a window for long periods of time just looking at rain fall on the ground. Such conduct would be considered odd in Ohio or Florida.

A SUMMER DAY AT GREER

A third source of Arizona's water supply after snow waters and runoff from desert cloudbursts is spring-fed streams such as the Little Colorado River, shown here in its early stages high up in the mountains at Greer. This is ideal trout fishing country, and the lakes and streams of eastern Arizona's high country are crowded with fishermen during the summer months. As we shall see later, this river undergoes a rather drastic change somewhere between this spot and its junction with the full-fledged Colorado River in the Grand Canyon. In fact, the sparkling clear mountain brook we see here would not merit the name Chiquito Colorado ("Little Red") if it kept this appearance throughout its course. However, it is fated to meet the desert, and not many miles downstream, at that. Deserts have a habit of affecting things that come in contact with them—vegetation, animals, human beings, and, especially, rivers.

(Photograph by Frank Elmer)

"TOO THICK TO DRINK . . .

. . . and too thin to plow" is the term that was generally used to describe the waters of the Colorado River before it was tamed by man. Now the words certainly apply to its tributary, the Little Colorado River as seen here near Holbrook and the Petrified Forest. This is the way we remember the real Colorado River ("Big Red") in the days before Hoover Dam. The contrast of the clear blue waters of Lake Mead and the river below the dam is a dramatic one. For this reason a great many of us in this state do not take kindly to the pathos and hand wringing of those who attack dams and lakes as affronts to the ecology. There is something fine and beautiful in the concept of falling water doing the work of producing electrical energy as contrasted to the burning of fossil fuels. The conservationists, who are to be otherwise warmly applauded except for this one blind spot, have been eminently successful in blocking additional power dams on the Colorado, and the giant smokestacks are now rising in the desert!

HOOVER DAM—THE GREAT EQUALIZER

Four decades have passed since this graceful concrete structure took form in Black Canyon, but its sight thrills me anew each time I see it. As a boy growing up in Kingman, the town in Arizona closest to the construction site, I was able to see it grow, block by block, until that great day arrived when the diversion gates were closed and Lake Mead began to form in the desert. It was called Boulder Dam in those days, and Kingman, needless to say, boasted a huge cloth banner stretched across Front Street proclaiming "Best Town by a Dam Site." Since completion, millions of visitors have descended into the dam's interior to view the huge penstock pipes and gleaming power plant.

While the obvious by-product of the dam is electrical energy, the main purpose for construction was protection of downstream areas from disastrous flooding, such as the breakthrough near Yuma in 1905 that formed the 400 square mile inland lake known to us now as the Salton Sea. The once wild and savage Colorado River, "Big Red," is now tamed by four great dams. But it was this one that led the way to first tame those muddy waters.

LONDON BRIDGE IS GOING UP!

On October 10, 1971, London Bridge, transported stone by stone from the Thames to the Arizona desert, was formally dedicated at Lake Havasu City by Sir Peter Studd, Lord Mayor of London and Jack Williams, Governor of Arizona. This bridge was a youngster, as things go in England—only about 140 years old, in fact. It was a good bridge, but the design that was more than adequate at its 1831 opening just could not cope with twentieth-century traffic into the City of London. The bridge was offered for sale to the highest bidder, who turned out to be the McCulloch Oil Corporation of California, designer of new planned communities, including Lake Havasu City. Robert McCulloch surmised that this famed span would serve as a centerpiece to his new city by the blue lake, and the steadily rising torrent of visitors indicates that he judged well. Tourists came to gawk in disbelief at the thousands of granite stones stored in a fenced yard as the world's greatest jigsaw puzzle. They could not get over the sight of those stones being put together again on dry land (a convenient way to build a bridge!) until the waters of Lake Havasu were brought to the bridge via a new channel. The Corporation of the City of London was given an acre of land by the bridge, on which was constructed The City of London Arms, a most handsome pub which has quickly become the leading dispenser of Watney's beer between Chicago and Los Angeles.

London Bridge seems to fit in well at its new desert home, and is even losing a bit of its grime under the Arizona sun. When an observer expressed concern that the bridge might become too clean and not seem authentic for that reason, the classic response came from Robert Beresford, the young British engineer in charge of the rebuilding project. "If that should happen," muttered Beresford morosely, "some Yank will be right around with his antiquing kit."

THE SILVERY COLORADO

Arizona's western border with California is marked by a string of clear, blue lakes formed by dams, with stretches of river water connecting them. These sections of the Colorado River also run clear and blue, ideal locations for water recreation sports. The area shown here lies below Parker Dam and above the city of Parker, Arizona. Weekend homes and trailer camps line these fifteen miles but an increasing number of year 'round residents have quite substantial houses.

These waters are also the site of an annual exciting boat race called the Parker Enduro, featuring dozens of power boats charging all out through the narrow canyons that line much of the river at this point. Mechanical dropouts are great in number, rivaling or exceeding the Indianapolis "500" in this respect. When the checkered flag falls, however, the silvery Colorado is returned to the more gentle attentions of water skiers, fishermen and boaters for yet another year.

A FIRE IN THE LAND—SUNSET CRATER

The volcanic origin of much of northern Arizona is brought home in a forceful manner at this grotesque landscape of jumbled lava flow a short distance northeast of Flagstaff. The big excitement that formed Sunset Crater took place only yesterday as geologic events are measured, the exact date being 1066 A.D. from a tree ring comparison system developed at the University of Arizona. The name was bestowed by Major John Wesley Powell, heroic one-armed conqueror of the Colorado River through the Grand Canyon. The major was impressed, as are modern-day visitors, by the cinder cone's coloration, ranging downward from the summit through shades of yellow, orange, reds and finally black ash at the base.

The young and vigorous climb a powdery trail to the summit, a kind of one step forward and two steps backward operation, while their elders are content to explore perpetual ice caves near the base, caves which reportedly supplied Flagstaff saloons in bygone days. The view towards the west from Sunset Crater is a remarkable one, traversing vast fields of desolate volcanic ash and culminating in the massive bulk of the San Francisco Peaks, volcanic creations themselves and Arizona's crowning point at 12,670 feet.

NATURE'S AIR CONDITIONING

This is where Arizona's citizens head when the dog days of summer are upon them. Almost half of the state is high country, complete with pine forests and cool breezes, as evidenced by this view of Tonto National Forest east of Payson. It is taken from atop the Mogollon Rim, which serves as a dramatic division point between northern and southern Arizona. It is the home country of Zane Grey, who wrote his all-time best seller *Under the Tonto Rim* not far from this spot.

Construction of superhighways leading to the pines has resulted in a vast increase in summer homes in the White Mountains and Flagstaff area, with many breadwinners commuting to Phoenix daily or several times each week. The availability of nature's air conditioning close at hand, plus the marvels of mechanical refrigeration, have removed much of the stigma of summer in Arizona. Nevertheless, I don't think there is a single Phoenician who wouldn't admit that he's glad when the brisk days of October roll around once more.

(Photograph by Frank Elmer)

DOWN ON THE BLUE

Each resident of Arizona has his definition of the single most scenic and picturesque place in the state. Mine is the valley of the Blue River, 'way over there by the New Mexico line south of Alpine, Arizona. Needless to say, it is reached only by a dirt road, for I can't imagine any place accessible by paved roads qualifying. A few ranchers live down on the Blue, and there is even a tiny post office, which we are told dates back to November 3, 1898.

The road through the canyon of the Blue River winds its merry way through fields of sunflowers, past beaver dams, and eventually climbs the western side of the canyon to meet US 666, The Coronado Trail, as it travels down the eastern backbone of Arizona. This view typifies, I believe, the hundreds of beautiful out of the way places that are waiting for the traveler who is willing to get off the beaten track and really explore Arizona. Yes, ma'am, there is more to Arizona than a traffic jam on Central Avenue in Phoenix on a smoggy afternoon!

(Photograph by Frank Elmer)

HIGH-ALTITUDE GOLF

Eastern visitors are beginning to discover the pleasures of Arizona in the summertime, much to their surprise and the mystification of their neighbors. A Chicago businessman, for example, can run out to O'Hare, catch a morning flight to Phoenix, drive his rental car to the golf course shown here at Alpine, Arizona, and get in a round of golf, all on the same day! The altitude here is 8,500 feet, which solves the temperature problem, the setting among pine and aspen forests is magnificent, and the pace of life is slow and easy. One reason for the leisurely pace is the altitude—you don't run around fast for very long up there and a golf cart is a welcomed accessory. But a much more important reason lies in the basic approach towards the game at this facility. There is no such thing as a starting time, the course is uncrowded, and family participation is encouraged. Somehow, I like to think that this is the way the game was meant to be played.

MOTHER NATURE'S BIG SHOW

The desert in bloom is a sight that pleases tourists, who assume that it is like this *every* springtime. Grizzled desert rats know better, and marvel in the miracle that produces a big show like this just now and then. They remember this same spot before the rains came, and know just how bleak and barren it had appeared. Wildflower seeds by the countless billions had lain there, sometimes for many years, just waiting for exactly that right combination of temperatures, winds and moisture to suddenly burst forth in a dazzling display of beauty. The Beavertail Cactus, on the other hand, is a much more dependable performer, and can usually be counted upon to bring forth some blossoms that rank with the view of a coral atoll from the air as nature's most brilliant colors.

THE JOSHUA FOREST

In the family of desert plants found throughout half of Arizona, the Joshua Tree is the one that best deserves the title "grotesque." No true cactus, but rather a member of the lily clan, the Joshuas of Arizona, Nevada, and California attract as many tourist cameras as the mighty Saguaros. Nowhere in these deserts do the Joshuas grow as thickly nor to such heights as in the place shown here, the road to Pierce Ferry northwest of Kingman, Arizona. When the plants bear white blossoms in late springtime, the effect on this landscape is almost as if a freak snowshower had covered the land with a mantle of white. The rugged cliffs in the background are called Grand Wash Cliffs and mark the start of the Grand Canyon when approached from the west. This is also the locale for yet another new Arizona planned community of the future, Meadview. The good citizens of Meadview, as the name implies, not only enjoy a view of Lake Mead, far below their high plateau home, but also see sunset on the Grand Wash Cliffs. That's scenic living!

SAGUARO—KING OF THE DESERT

When it comes to choosing the dominant form in the Arizona desert it's strictly no contest. The incredible saguaro cactus wins on all counts—size, grace, longevity, and even for its waxy white blossom, which is Arizona's state flower. One of the basic articles of faith to good Arizonans is the belief that a photograph showing a saguaro, if made in the United States of America, is in Arizona and nowhere else. It is a strange quirk of nature and man's rather arbitrary establishment of state boundary lines that causes this to be so, for why should these giants of the desert grow right up to the Colorado River and not beyond? From time to time I hear rumors that a stray saguaro or two has been found in some secluded draw around Blythe or Earp, both of which are in the great state of California. I would like to believe these tales are false, and will so believe until that time when I am taken there to see with my own eyes. In this view is a glimpse of Apache Lake on the Apache Trail leading to Theodore Roosevelt Dam. The saguaros shown here are probably around 150 years of age.

74

WHERE NEVER IS HEARD A DISCOURAGING WORD

The cowboy is still very much a part of the Arizona scene, whether out on a working cattle ranch doing the jobs cowboys did a century ago or, as in this case, getting dudes acquainted with their horses prior to a morning ride at a Wickenburg guest ranch. Wickenburg, about 50 miles northwest of Phoenix, dubs itself "Dude Ranch Capital of the World," and has no serious contenders to this title. The ranch shown here, Remuda Ranch, is the oldest of all Arizona guest ranches, dating back to the 1920s. The horse is an important part of this life, of course, and the tenderfoot rider usually needs some words of assurance. "We'll give you old Star, here," the wrangler will mumble. "Star ain't never been ridden, so you'll start out together."

THEY WENT THATAWAY!

Hollywood's producers have long used Arizona's scenic areas for location shooting, particularly Oak Creek Canyon, Monument Valley and the desert areas near Tucson. A few permanent sets have sprung up, such as Apacheland, shown here, which is located just a few miles east of Apache Junction in the shadows of famed Superstition Mountain. At regular intervals actors stage bank holdups for the benefit of tourists, complete with much loud gunfire. Black Bart invariably bites the dust and the lawman emerges unscathed, which is as it should be. Old Tucson, west of modern Tucson, was first built as a set for a movie entitled, simply, *Arizona*. The story by Clarence Buddington Kelland told of Miss Phoebe Titus, who baked pies in Tucson about a century ago, a kind of early day Mildred Pierce. The production year was 1940, and Phoebe's role was played by Jean Arthur. The set was retained, and has grown greatly, most recently serving as the site for TV's very successful series *High Chaparral*. Meanwhile, up in colorful Oak Creek Canyon, photographer Bob Bradshaw has built a western town set on his ranch, and Southwest Studios constructed a modern sound stage north of Scottsdale that was used by Arizona resident Dick Van Dyke for his television show. And, of course, way up there by the Utah border, in Monument Valley, John Ford has continued to shoot pictures just because he likes the place. In some cases the red dirt and towering buttes don't figure in the plot, but this doesn't faze the director, whose favorite lookout spot on the valley rim now bears the name Ford Point.

SUPAI RODEO

The rodeo in Arizona comes in many forms, including a big one at Phoenix which is staged in air-conditioned comfort within the confines of a room that otherwise features ice hockey, automobile shows and the Phoenix Suns basketball team. The one shown here, in the Grand Canyon home of the Havasupai Indian Tribe, lacks seats, air conditioning, candy butchers and public address system. It is by far the more enjoyable of the two. The Supais are great cowboys, and invite members of other tribes into the canyon for this annual rodeo primarily as a means for extracting some prize money from their red brothers. It usually works, for members of this small tribe invariably draw down a disproportionate share of rodeo money when competing in large events such as the All-Indian Pow-Wow at Flagstaff. They are born riders, and it is not uncommon to see a full-grown horse being ridden by a lone Supai cowboy aged four or five years. While air conditioning may be lacking, the opening parade of riders matches for thrills anything staged by members of the professional rodeo show circuit. It's not fast and it's not fancy—just a double row of Indian cowboys riding past in silence and dignity, following their country's flag held high by the leader.

WATER IN THE LAND

The fruitful desert can be seen in many parts of Arizona as water is brought to the arid land and it prospers. This is a land of year 'round growing season and heavy yield, IF the water is there. First evidence of irrigation by ditches and canals was found in the Salt River Valley around Phoenix when remains of prehistoric diggings of the Hohokam peoples were unearthed. Major canals have existed around Phoenix since the 1890s, but it was construction of Theodore Roosevelt Dam on the Salt River in 1911 that really laid the ground-work for the vast system of irrigated farming in Arizona today. The irrigation waters are thoroughly used, but it has been necessary to supplement them with pumped water from wells that grow deeper and deeper each year. As the water table continues to drop pumping becomes more expensive and we may someday see some crop lands return to the desert. A great Central Arizona Project is now underway that will pump water all the way from Lake Havasu on the state's western boundary to the Phoenix area. It will help, but the long-range future of agriculture in this desert land is still somewhat in doubt.

THE ANCIENT ONES

Casa Grande Ruins National Monument near Coolidge is a relic from the days of "The Ancient Ones," the Hohokam people who built this remarkable apartment house on the flat desert floor, created an advanced system of irrigation canals in what is now the Phoenix area, and then mysteriously disappeared from the scene hundreds of years ago. We are not yet sure of the purpose of this adobe structure—perhaps lookout post, storage room, living quarters, or some combination of these. Whatever its reason, Casa Grande, "The Big House," is quite an achievement. Since adobe melts in the rain, a huge steel canopy was erected for future protection of the main building and outlying walls were stabilized with cement. Casa Grande is somewhat off the main tourist trails, but is a worthy subject for a detour en route to Tucson or Phoenix. The other Indian ruins in Arizona were inhabited by known peoples, whose descendants still reside in the area. Not so in the case of the Hohokam, however—they are lost and gone forever.

SAN XAVIER DEL BAC—WHITE DOVE OF THE DESERT

If Arizona has one building more notable than any other, one link with the first advent of the white man into this region, it must be Mission San Xavier del Bac a few miles south of Tucson. The year of that first contact was 1692, and it was made by Fr. Eusebio Kino, a Jesuit. The mission at Bac flourished and waned during the Jesuit days, while contending with a constant threat of the savage Apache. The Jesuits were forced to leave the New World in 1767, and their missions were given over to the Franciscans, notably, in the case of Bac, to Fr. Francisco Garces. The present building was completed in 1797 and has continued to this day to serve as a house of worship for the Papago Indians who live about it. It is a place of great color, and dazzling brilliance. Here there is much joy and laughter, and it is a fine place to be for even a few moments. Unlike many California missions that now find themselves hemmed in by downtown buildings, Bac sits alone in the flat fields of the Papago. It is a scene not too different from that of 1797.

BOOM AND BUST

Arizona's ghost towns, too numerous to mention by name, are all monuments
to the hard rock miners—to their hard work, determination, and, above all,
their incredible optimism. This weathered shack and battered safe were found
at White Hills, between Kingman and Hoover Dam in northwestern Arizona's
Mohave County. This was a great silver camp in the 1890s, with a population
of 1,500 souls. By the turn of the century it was well on its way towards oblivion,
leaving behind ruins of a 20-stamp mill, a long row of sagging wooden buildings
and monumental piles of beer barrel hoops and whiskey bottles. Today, White
Hills is the classic ghost town—no curio shops, no grizzled prospector posing
with white burro, no people at all. It's the way a ghost town ought to be.

TOMBSTONE, ARIZONA TERRITORY

"The Town Too Tough to Die" is alive and well down in Cochise County. The imposing structure shown here served as the county court house for nearly a half century and is now a treasured landmark and museum in the Arizona State Park system. Tombstone was brought back to life by a television show and now serves as a magnet drawing visitors from all over the world. They aren't disappointed when they get there, either, for the entire town seems to be a living museum of frontier life. Here one can freely walk the board sidewalks that felt the boots of Doc Holliday, Wyatt Earp and the Clantons, even though entry into the noted O.K. Corral area involves a slight fee. There's Boot Hill, the pioneer territorial newspaper still published as *The Tombstone Epitaph*, an opera house reminding all that Tombstone was once larger than San Francisco, and the remarkable Lady Banksia rose tree filling a half block. Towering above them all, however, is this fine old Victorian court house, the pride of Tombstone, Arizona Territory.

THE OLD PUEBLO

Tucson, Arizona's second city, blends a strong heritage of Spanish and Mexican influence with the modern steel and glass appearance of an American city. The settlement was first seen by Fr. Kino in 1697, and a small pueblo with church and wall for defense was constructed here by Fr. Francisco Garces in 1769. Tucson remained under Mexican rule until sale of this area to the United States by the Gadsden Purchase in 1853. The flavor of this Latin background is found throughout Tucson today in its Spanish architecture, extensive use of Spanish street names, and in an attitude towards life that seems somehow more relaxed than that found in the capital city to the north. Tucson is a university town, a major military base and a world-renowned center for astronomical research. It also serves as Arizona's primary trade center with our neighbor to the south, Sonora, and continues its role as a haven for winter visitors. The modern trappings of growth can be seen in Tucson's downtown center but its residents are determined that it always remain The Old Pueblo.

PHOENIX FROM THE ASHES

The sparkling jet-propelled capital city of Arizona is little more than one hundred years old, rising truly like the Phoenix bird on the site of an ancient and long-vanished Hohokam civilization. This view is made from the brand-new Phoenix Civic Plaza convention hall and music theatre, looking towards the state's dominant structure, Valley Center, home base for the Valley National Bank, largest in the Rocky Mountain region. As Phoenix and its suburbs near the one million mark, a tightrope balancing act is required to equate the factors of metro growth with the easy pace of desert living that brought most of the million people here in the first place. This adjustment is still being accomplished in fairly good order, and the citizens of Phoenix are devoting an ever-increasing attention to the preservation of their way of life. It is a manner of living well worth the effort to preserve.

94